LET'S TALK PUSSY

LIVES DEPEND ON IT

ALETHEA TAYLOR

LET'S TALK PUSSY
LIVES DEPEND ON IT

ALETHEA TAYLOR

Alethea Taylor, LLC
Philadelphia, PA

ALETHEA TAYLOR

Helping You Unlock Your Potential

ISBN (Paperback): 978-1-7334452-1-4

Library of Congress Control Number: 2021912750

Printed in The United States

Alethea Taylor, LLC
Philadelphia, PA 19111-4567
www.info@aletheataylor.com

Visit the author's website at www.AletheaTaylor.com

What unites every female in the world also represents their greatest threat. To save girls and women everywhere, it's time to take a stand and speak candidly about this very personal and powerful bond.

TABLE OF CONTENTS

ACKNOWLEDGEMENTS

Giving praises to my **Lord and Savior, Jesus Christ,** from whom all blessings flow. Without Him, I can do nothing, but with Him, all things are possible. Thank you, God, for loving, protecting, and blessing me.

To my mother, **Nancy,** I love you dearly. Thank you for instilling in me the confidence to do whatever I set my mind to. Thank you, Mom, for being a strong, positive female influence in my life and for demonstrating how to persevere every day. Thank you for being my rock, my support, my cheerleader, and for believing in me, sharing your knowledge with me, and pushing me to do all I could do to fulfill my greatest potential. I thank you for loving me beyond measure and showing me how to love myself completely. I find so much joy in knowing that you believe in me, that you continue to speak life over me, and encourage me to keep going. Most of all, Mom, thank you for being my mother, my friend, my comfort, and my security. I appreciate and love you beyond measure!

To my late father, **James,** I'm proud to call you my father. You supported me, loved me, and was always there for me. All the advice you gave me I recall and treasure as it guides me through life! I miss you, Dad. I love you and carry you in my heart every day. I'm grateful to God for the many years we had together, and most of all, I'm thankful to God for giving me a wonderful father like you!

To my sister, **Melinda,** my ride or die. Thank you for always having my back! You are my sister, my best friend, and I love you dearly! You always push me, support me, pray for me, and speak life over me! There's nothing you wouldn't do for me. Thank you! You are a beautiful woman and queen! God has blessed me above and beyond when he made you, my sister!

To my brother, **Blain,** thank you for your love, your support, and your persistence in pushing me to following my dreams and to see them come to fruition. Your encouragement, support, and continuous check-in with me regarding the status of any goal or project keeps me on track and persevering forward. Thank you for believing in me. I love you dearly.

Thank you to my four-legged baby boy, my "son" **Keno**. I'm thankful to you for the time you demand for walks and playtime and just quiet time together. It's because of you that I find balance and take the time to pause and enjoy life. You bring me so much joy. Mommy loves you so much!

To my editor, **Diana,** I am grateful for you, not only for your help editing this book, but for your willingness to be part of this project. Thanks so much for your honesty, feedback, and for sharing your thoughts, experiences, and insight. Your assistance and counsel were invaluable; thank you!

To my friend **Jessica** and my sister **Lindy**, thank you both for being the first people to read the book and for providing your feedback. I appreciate the time you spend to lend a second set of eyes and for your support. I love you, ladies.

Lastly, there are so many other **friends** and **family** members who continue to support and encourage me. To those of you who continue to support me, believed in me, encourage me, and most of all love me, I am so grateful for all of you. I've been blessed with the greatest support system anyone could pray for.

1 Thessalonians 5:11 "Therefore encourage one another and build each other up, just as you are already doing."

PREFACE

It is my true passion and heart's desire to help girls and women grow to a level of confidence and strength. Over the years, I had the pleasure of mentoring, supporting, and encouraging females of all ages. And, as I continue to be blessed with the gift of growing older and learning from many life experiences, particularly concerning relationships, I feel an even stronger desire, responsibility, and obligation to share my experiences, and wisdom to help women recognize their worth, value, and relationship choices.

As much as I take joy in helping others acknowledge their worth and believe that I deliver this advice with the utmost transparency, I recently questioned if I was real enough with those who sought my wisdom or with those I had an obligation to share with. This uncertainty crept into my mind the second time I spent over two hours trying to help a 23-year-old woman tackle the heartache she was experiencing because she felt that the young man she was involved with wanted her only for sex. During our first conversation, I shared my relationship experiences, gave her things to think about, and helped her address her challenges.

By the time we ended our conversation, she felt better, more confident, and empowered to move forward and end things with the young man. However, that was short-lived. One month later, I awoke to a phone call at 1 a.m. from the same young woman crying hysterically. Initially, I thought she was hurt, but thank God she wasn't. She was devastated by the same young man we discussed a month earlier.

As soon as she whispered his name, all I could think of was, *I failed her!* Silently, I wondered why she would cry over the same young man, particularly after I gave her what I believed was solid advice. Nonetheless, she shared that she surrendered again to his alluring smile, smell, and his, "je ne sais quoi", leaving her even more miserable than before. Again, he phoned late at night wanting and needing to see her, to talk to her, and that all he needed was to be with her, which would make everything right in his life. She said the stress in his voice and his apparent state of desperation was something she couldn't ignore, and despite her instincts that screamed against it, she couldn't resist and eventually jumped into rescue mode. She convinced herself that something was different about his demeanor, or should I say his deception, and after succumbing to her feeble resistance toward seeing him, she eventually said, "Yes, come, come. I'll be waiting for you."

When he arrived, his distress, desperation, and even sadness immediately disappeared when she opened the door. Of course, she chalked that up to his happiness in seeing her, however, within moments, he jumped into his regular routine of: "I'm hungry.", What do you have to drink?", and "I'm horny as hell." He immediately grabbed her, led her to the sofa, bent her over, pulled her tights and panties down, and roughly and quickly, as she described it, "He began to fuck me!" She hated how he handled her, but she didn't stop him.

Instead, she remained bent over the sofa gripping the arm to brace herself against his animalistic thrusting that became harder and harder. With each mindless thrust, she felt she was vanishing, diminishing, and just as he reached the point of orgasm, she was heartbroken because she felt like she was nothing more than a warm body to be used merely to release the pleasure he so desired. She realized that his presence had nothing to do with her at all. It was simply about his need for sex. She secretly shed a tear.

She never told him how empty, unfulfilling, and dehumanized she felt. She wanted him to leave but had no idea how to tell him. However, she didn't have to think of how to tell him to leave because seconds after he climaxed, he made a quick trip to the bathroom to freshen up, browsed her kitchen cabinets to grab a quick snack, looked at this phone, and then said, "Sorry, I just got a text. I have to bounce." As she watched him walk out the door, she shared, "I just knotted my head because I couldn't say anything without bursting into tears."

As she told her story, I thought, *I let her down.* Was I negligent with my advice to her? I was sure my initial advice would help her avoid another pitfall with the same young man, but maybe she gave everything she had. Maybe it was my advice that failed her. Nevertheless, I felt like I wasn't reaching this young woman, that nothing I said truly rooted in her mind. I questioned if she was ever educated about her pussy, if she was miseducated about her pussy, and if anyone ever sat down with her to talk to her about her pussy. Did she attend the lame sex education class offered in schools that focused superficially on anatomy but failed to address the true issues regarding education about sex?

The failure to go beyond the function of the "vagina", particularly during puberty, is a failure at the most essential time in a young girl's life. Did I do the same thing? Did I provide candy-coated, superficial advice that failed to dispel the myths and misconceptions clouding her judgment and failed to create a "wow", or realization, moment? Was I too careful about how I spoke to her about her vagina versus her pussy? Did her mother, grandmother, aunt, or any other mother figure sit down and speak to her about her pussy? Fortunately for me, I was blessed to have a mother who understood the need to educate, prepare, and equip her daughters with the knowledge not only about their vagina but the very desired, sought-after, pleasurable organ that we possessed — our pussy.

I recall one Halloween night when I was 10 years old. I went out with all my siblings, cousins, and friends trick or treating. We spent a few hours roaming through the neighborhood having a wonderful time. As the night ended, I couldn't wait to get back to my aunt's house where my parents waited for me to tell them how much fun I had. When I entered the house, I was so excited! I wanted to show my mother all the candy I got, so I yelled for her. I rushed past my father, ran to my mother, gave her my bag of candy, and ran to the bathroom.

My excitement and happiness soon transformed into a horror story for me. I remember looking at the toilet tissue saturated with blood and screaming as loudly as I could because I thought I was dying. My mother ran to my rescue and quickly reassured me that I wasn't dying and that I'd just gotten my period, something that all females experienced. She explained to me what I had to do from that point. That was the quick and short story I received at my aunt's house. However, over the next several days, my mother lectured me about my responsibilities because I'd physically, if not mentally, become a "woman". She told me how to care for my vagina, not to let anyone touch my vagina, or persuade me to let them do anything to my vagina. And while I didn't fully comprehend my mother's words, it was my mother's fear and concern that prompted me to heed those responsibilities.

When I was 13, my mother sat me down once again, but this time, I was ready to receive the advice that advanced me from the basics about my vagina to the stark realities of having a PUSSY! My mother also needed my sister and me to understand that pussy was something strongly sought after, yearned for, and desired, and we had an enormous responsibility to understand all the nuances of its ownership. My mother didn't play with words because she had to protect us. To do that, she had to educate us in plain language.

My friends' mothers or female family members referred to their vaginas as "your cookie". They said things like, "Take care of your cookie." I never understood the analogy to a cookie, because when I thought of a cookie, I thought of a delicious treat that I always shared with others. I remember asking my mother, "Why do so many people call the vagina "Your cookie?" She explained that "Cookie" wasn't a reference to our vagina but to how our pussy was considered a sweet treat many would want us to share. And while many did consider it a treat, she emphasized that what we had was definitely not a cookie. She didn't want us growing up with such an immature belief. What we had was a pussy, not a cookie! It wasn't meant to be shared but protected from threats we had yet to learn about because people would do anything to get what we had. She didn't want us to be abused, raped, or molested for what we had. She didn't want us used, sold, or prostituted for what we had. She had to prepare her girls for the real world because the real world wouldn't take pity on us or go easy on us. The real world would be coming for us, and we HAD to know what to expect. Young or not, too much information too soon or not, we had to know.

I remember a time shortly after the pussy conversation with my mother. I was playing a game of kickball with some friends, and it was my turn to kick the ball, but before I did, a boy challenged me. He said, "I'll bet you can't kick a home run." I replied, "If I win, you have to buy me a juice and a box of Jolly Joes." He replied, "If you don't, you have to show me your pussy!" All the other boys started laughing and shouting, "Oh, no!" I was surprised by his response, particularly because he was only 11. I immediately responded, "No way, you nasty thing!" And as I think back, this boy and others around his age already knew about pussy. He didn't say, "vagina", he referred to my vagina as "pussy". He knew! But sadly, I think I was the only girl who knew. Thanks to my parents, I was prepared for his response, but unfortunately, my girlfriends were clueless.

That is when I recalled my conversation with my father. While my mother educated my sister and me about pussy, my father also prepared us for the world we would face as women, particularly regarding tricks like this boy tried with me to get to my pussy. My father's conversation with me was quite different from my mother's, but it educated me about what I heard from the boy, if not more. My father acknowledged that he was aware that my mother already talked to me, but he wanted to offer another perspective for me to consider. With a serious demeanor and his soothing baritone voice, he spoke carefully but lovingly, about the reality of the world I would face.

During our conversation, he never uttered the word "pussy". He told me how a young man should treat me, speak to me, and respect me, and that boys, young men, and even adult men would say things or use tricks or games to try to touch me. He told me how I should use my voice and shout "NO" and call them out just as I did with that boy that day. He added that even more importantly, there would be predators who would pursue me, men who would try to use me, and how to recognize them. He also emphasized that I should always tell him or my mother if anyone ever made me feel uncomfortable or tried to persuade me not to tell anybody what they tried to do. He ended our conversation by telling me how much he loved me and that I was beautiful, something both my parents always told me and my sister. Their words always left me feeling very much loved. As I grew older, I realized how important each of my parents' conversations, guidance, and advice helped me navigate the waters of life as a woman.

And as I continued my conversation with the young woman, the conversations I had with my partners continued to come to me, particularly, my conversations with my mother. As much as I appreciated my father's advice, what my mother gave me was something only a woman could give. It was raw, incredibly honest, eye-opening, and from a place of experience. What she bestowed on my sister and me was invaluable. Because of my mother, I learned at an early age that my vagina was more than just about a monthly period, tampons, pads, or where babies came from. I learned that the soft, warm, and wet place I possessed would be sought after and that I had to be prepared for threats seen and unseen to protect myself and my pussy.

As this young woman shared her disappointment and hurt with me, I thought I'd done the same for her. I was sure I told her about her vagina. I was even more certain that I failed to tell her about her pussy. That's when I realized that more often than not, those pursuing the pussy know more about it than its owners.

I found myself frustrated but awakened to the realization that if I wanted to help this young woman and many others facing the same situation, heartache, and unawareness, I had to get real. And by real, I mean REAL like my mother was with me, meaning no sugar-coated words. It is my duty to educate and help women understand what they possess but to do that, they must first understand the ESSENCE of the pussy and then the importance of caring for it, protecting it, and most of all, understanding that they are more than pussy!

INTRODUCTION

As a young girl growing up, do you recall being told what it meant to be a girl? Were you told about how you should behave as a young girl? Did anyone talk to you about your body and the changes you would experience as you grew older? Was your menstrual cycle a surprise to you, or were you prepared for the day you saw the blood dripping from your vagina? Did anyone ever discuss your vagina, how to care for it, and recognize any symptoms such as odor, itching, burning, physical changes, and what to do if you did? Or did you learn about your vagina on your own? Did anyone feel comfortable enough to tell you that yes, you have a vagina, but what you possessed was a pussy? Yes, a pussy is quite different from your vagina.

This important difference is why we fail our girls when we continue to talk only in terms of "vagina". Our unwillingness to talk about pussy or have critical conversations about pussy has led to widespread ignorance about pussy. Like it or not, what we hold between our legs, nestled in our panties, is far more than a vagina. The vagina is the nucleus of the body, but the pussy is the hub of desire and pleasure. The vagina is the gateway to planting life, but the pussy is the pleasure zone that provides many an escape from the stresses and pressures of life. The vagina is the mothership to deliver life, but the pussy is something so sought-after that a woman's life can be jeopardized because of it. The vagina is a spout for monthly cleansing, but the pussy can be an incubator for diseases to thrive and can threaten life.

If you're one of many girls who were told growing up only about the distinction that girls have a vagina and boys have a penis instead of girls having a vagina that's perceived as a pussy, you were cheated of essential information all young women should be aware of — that you have both a vagina and a pussy.

Maybe no one told you about your pussy because those around you who were knowledgeable about the pussy couldn't have necessary conversations simply because they were uncomfortable using the word, pussy. Yes, pussy is a word that's considered vulgar, derogatory, demeaning, and even taboo, but to some, a sexual turn-on to keep hidden. We want to gasp, mutter under our breath, and give dirty looks when we say, "pussy" out loud. However, we cannot allow the word to have such power over us that we shy away from telling our girls, our daughters, our sisters, and all other females the truth — that they have a pussy, one of the most desired and pleasurable parts of the female body.

We need to remove the stigma from the word and move to a natural and necessary adaptation of "pussy". Therefore, we must take control of the word because our girls' lives depend on it. While we allow the word to control us rather than control the word, a girl or woman is being raped right now by a stranger or family member for her pussy. While we are uncomfortable or embarrassed to hear the word spoken, a teenage girl is being trafficked for her pussy. While some may whisper their disapproval of my use of the word "pussy", young girls, teenagers, and women are being abused, sold, and prostituted for their pussy. While we act so appalled by the use of the word, our girls and young women are showcased in a catalog like merchandise for their pussy. While we fidget uncomfortably or display disgust about using the word pussy, millions illegally sell and profit from pussy.

Are we uncomfortable using the word pussy? When we speak it, we speak with a sense of embarrassment and concern about others hearing us. The shame of it all! However, when we use the word in certain situations, we speak it with such vigor, power, and conviction. People pay for it, rape for it, traffic it, but we don't want to talk about pussy? We play with it, talk to it, name it, and spend so much money on products for it, but we're afraid to call it by its powerful name, "pussy". We love the power, the lure, and the thrill of talking about pussy. We feel good about the word when we text our sexual partners. And who has ever said, "I can't wait for you to get this vagina". No, we say or text, "I can't wait for you to get this pussy!" Have you ever told your sexual partner that your vagina is wet and waiting for them, or did you say that your pussy is wet and waiting for them? When having sex, has your partner ever asked you, "Who's vagina is this?" Or did they ask, "Who's pussy is this?" Let's be real. We can use the word for our own satisfaction, but what about helping someone else?

While more are worried about the utterance of "pussy", they conveniently ignore the urgency of teaching girls and teens everywhere to fully understand the need to value and protect their pussy. We need to be uncomfortable about the lack of information, misinformation, and absence of truthful and honest conversations that our girls so rightfully deserve and need to hopefully avoid the pitfalls, the agony, and the hurt that can negatively affect, impact, and possibly plague their lives for a long time or even forever, simply because we surrender our power to the word instead of claiming power over it. Let's not continue to consider the word dirty because pussy is such a beautiful, lively, and important part of the female body, yet we are ashamed to call it by its name.

Let's not surrender to the negative connotation, but a willingness to call it what it is, because by doing so, we can empower girls and women to help them gain the confidence to control their pussy, and gain the critical knowledge necessary to assume the responsibilities that come with having a pussy and being caretakers of that pussy.

Ladies, we owe it to our girls to help them in every way possible. We cannot skip the pussy conversation simply because we are worried about "the crudeness" of using the word pussy versus vagina. We must be more concerned about not delivering the harsh truth about their pussy versus their vagina. People are watching and waiting for the right opportunity to take advantage of them because they know the value of what our girls and young women carry between their legs.

They need to know! They cannot possess the golden treasure without knowing the value of that treasured possession when everyone else knows more than them simply because no one wanted to talk about pussy. Newsflash! You can avoid or delegate a task, but you cannot delegate responsibility. We are all responsible for doing the right thing for our girls and young women. Otherwise, they remain dangerously unprepared for predators who will use them for nothing more than their pussy. Without knowing what to expect or how to handle themselves, girls and women won't know how to detect threats or how to protect themselves.

We put more emphasis on teaching our children how to drive than providing our girls vital information that could save their lives. We shy away from explaining the intricate details about their bodies and their pussy. If we say nothing, then we become accomplices to future threats. Yes, accomplices! Of course, we cannot control what a girl or woman will do, but we need to look back with certainty that we shared the truth, provided instruction, guidance, and advice that helped them on their way.

But as much as this call to educate our girls points the finger to women to do their part, fathers, uncles, and other male figures can also significantly contribute to the conversation. Men, you have a unique perspective you can share, tell, and add to the conversation, because as a man, your experience and the lens through which you view pussy, is different from a woman's perspective. You offer knowledge from a completely different perspective. You can advise females what to look out for regarding the games, tricks, and lies a man may tell them just to get to their pussy.

If you really want to be honest and real, which I prefer you do, you can share, whether right or wrong, how you've treated women, sought women, and used women for nothing more than their pussy. Are you concerned enough that your own daughters, sisters, friends, and female family members are adequately prepared for life? Prepared for the world for no other reason than they are females, and you know what's ahead of them? Men, you are not exempt from the conversation. You have to ask yourselves if you are failing your daughters or any other young woman in your life? Are you missing your opportunity, obligation, or responsibility as well? Let's not forget, it takes a village.

Please do not stand by and let another girl or woman become a victim. Would you rather be judged for saying the word pussy or doing nothing to help someone understand the pussy? Would you rather be judged as the person shouting the word rather than doing nothing to warn females of what they may face in the future because they have a pussy? Surely our girls and women deserve more from us than misplaced reluctance, embarrassment, or ignorance. Will you stand up, speak out, and pledge to support females? Will you help?

Are you ready to help? Are you ready to move beyond vagina to pussy? Are you ready to take control of the word? Are you comfortable with the word? Say it — pussy, pussy, pussy! Now that you have spoken the word, buckle up, and let's save a girl, teen, or woman from becoming prey or making catastrophic mistakes because we have not told them the truth or were afraid to tell them the truth.

Truth be Told, it's time to get real. Lives depend on it.

So, Let's Talk Pussy!

CHAPTER ONE

THE ESSENCE OF PUSSY

Sister-friends, if no one told you or were willing to tell you, I will. I will take the time to get real with you about your body and your pussy because your life depends on it! It's time to get real — no time to dance around the subject, share vague information, or shy away from the conversation. It's time for the truth! And the truth is, you have a pussy!

Ladies, you need to know!

All about the essence of pussy!

You need to know that because of who you are, what you possess, and your capability to provide unmeasurable pleasure, you need to know what lies ahead. You need to know that people will beat you, kidnap you, and sell you. People will abuse you, rape you, and molest you just to take what you have for their own pleasure — your pussy!

That's why you need to know everything about yourself as a female, particularly as it relates to your body! When you were a child, your parents were responsible for caring for you and protecting you. However, as you grew older, and the more you were exposed to the world, the more you needed to know to navigate a society filled with potential threats and hazards. While our upbringings instructed us in many things, this didn't always include the most important subjects about what you would face in life as a woman.

Unfortunately, not all of us received or will receive information that can protect us, and trying to figure things out without guidance is not good enough! You need cold, hard facts and conversations! And the cold, hard truth is, ladies, that you have a vagina, but you possess a pussy — a pleasurable and desired part of your body that people will stop at nothing to get!

It may seem confusing how the female body possesses both a vagina and pussy. However, it's really not that complicated.

The female body is a beautiful, complex multifaceted, nurturing, life-bearing, and pleasurable work of art. It is designed with unique parts and functionalities that men cannot duplicate nor perform. For example, a woman's breasts are used for nursing children and her own and another's pleasure. The center of her body between her legs is both the vagina and the pussy. The vagina is the entryway to the body, the organ that bleeds monthly, known as your period or menstrual cycle, and the passageway to delivering babies. However, the pussy is a pleasure zone, sex organ, and highly coveted.

Close your eyes and imagine sitting on the beach on a balmy 75-degree day while a fragrant breeze caresses your body. The waves gently lap just where your toes peek from the sand. With each wave, your feet slowly sink deeper into the sand, and all your stress, worries, and tension slowly ease away, creating the most sublime, relaxing, and pleasurable sensation. You surrender to the feeling and become so engulfed by the sensuous experience that all you can do is sigh.

Women, your pussy causes a person to sigh. However, it is such a powerful, intense, and physically satisfying experience that people will do anything to get it. Think of vacationers who pay a premium to experience the euphoria of paradise simply to relax and forget about the stress in their lives even for only a short time. This is the power of what you possess. Many will use and abuse you for it, try to steal it from you, or sell you for it. It's often referred to as "sunshine in a bottle". This is the reason why it's so important for you to know how to care for and protect your pussy!

But before you can truly care for or protect your pussy, you must understand the pussy and the very essence of the pussy. You need to know who and what pussy is.

Let's let Pussy speak for herself.

I am not your vagina. Your vagina has a completely different function than mine. I am your vagina's paternal twin, Pussy. Yes, Pussy! I am the soft, warm, moist, and inviting hole that provides the ultimate in pleasure, excitement, and sexual experience.

My essence is motivating, seductive, and a hypnotic siren's song.

LET'S TALK PUSSY | ALETHEA TAYLOR

I am wet, sticky, and moist. I am warm, welcoming, and pulsating.

I am the most yearned-for, desired, sought-after, lusted-for, and magnificent body part on Earth! I am what you long to touch, to feel, to play with. I am your fantasy, the essence of your daydreams. I am the thing that you cannot wait to get home to.

I can make you forget your troubles and ease your pain. You use me to take you on a journey to an alternate reality or your personal utopia. I take over your mind, your body, and your senses. Every cell, every nerve, surrenders to me.

I provide the most intense pleasure you can ever experience or imagine. You become my servant, ready and willing to obey my command.

I can make you lose control, succumb to my will, and even make you stupidly ask, who's Pussy is this?

When I say I am throbbing and need release, even if you are tired, I can command you to jump to your feet and run, skip, walk, or drive miles to have me.

My hot, engorged, wet flesh arouses and excites you. You slide your fingers deep inside me and savor the salty taste and intoxicating aroma of my juice. By now, your appetite is ravenous, and like a starving animal, you want only to bury your face on my succulent plate of juicy flesh and devour me. Once I allow you access, you eat and eat until you collapse, sated and delirious.

When you enter me, my walls grip you like a silken glove. You forget everything around you because I swaddle you in a veil of warm, pulsating, succulent flesh that sends your body into ecstasy.

And with every hungry thrust you make, I'm inhaling you, consuming you, and milking you to the point of explosion, but then I slow down. I toy with you, torment and tease you because I don't want you to release too soon. After all, I am in control. You are beyond rational thought or reason. Your body and mind are no longer your own. Only your instinct commands you, and that instinct is to obey.

When I straddle you and ride you like a pony, I control the pace, the course, and the flow of our encounter. You shout out my name like a warrior riding into battle. I grab you, hug you, and brand your flesh until every pore on your body quivers. I rev your engine like a race car or rocket ready to blast off. I make you cum with joy.

And when I'm finished with you, when your body is drained of energy the way a vampire sucks the blood of its victims, I let you sleep like a baby because that is what you have become.

I am, Pussy!

I am that source of pleasure so powerful and overwhelming that you will do anything to claim it, but since you can't, you take me, restrain me, and ship me off to strange places and people to collect money for the extreme pleasure I provide. But never once do you remember that I am also human and not a piece of merchandise to be bought and sold at the market!

I am so desirable, yet so vulnerable that you take advantage of the person I am. You lose your mind over me, but you retain enough cold calculation to understand that what you are about to do is wrong, but you don't care. I have become a commodity to you, and because you want me so badly, you don't care about stealing and corrupting my innocence. For a few minutes of pleasure, you will gladly alter the course of my life and cause untold pain without even a blink of remorse.

I am all you want, and you will do anything to get me. You will lie, cheat, steal, and even kill to possess me with no thought of the consequences.

You cannot wait to ram yourself deep inside me, thrusting until your eyes roll to the back of your head. I take you to the point of explosion while your body reacts as though you are suffering a seizure.

I am so desired that you dismiss the rest of my body as irrelevant except for my lips and mouth that you use for your own pleasure. You disregard my mind and my voice, but you claim my breasts and clitoris as your playground and use them for your enjoyment but often to my pain. Above all, you forget about my heart. You cannot see below the surface of the body that you regard as nothing but a toy.

I get you so excited that sometimes you want to enter me without protection or regard for any risk of disease because you only care about pleasure. But if I resist, if I speak out, you use force. Now, it's no longer about pleasure but about violence and control. You will take me any way you can because that is what *you* want.

I am, Pussy!

In short, the essence of pussy is pleasure. Utopia. Paradise. But it can also be pain. Purgatory. Hell.

But the truth is that your pussy is yours! It is far more than just a part of your body. It is the essence of your womanhood, a symbol of your femininity. Even if you have not taken the time to think about your pussy, someone else is, now, today, and tomorrow. Because of this, you must guard your pussy like the treasure it is. You are its rightful owner. You are the key holder.

And like anything valuable, you must do everything to protect your pussy.

CHAPTER TWO

NO ONE TOLD ME

When you are ignorant to important information, the encounters, situations, people, and your family history can affect and influence your life in ways you never imagined. However, you have the power to change your life and influence positive change in the lives of others. Take a stand and break this vicious cycle!

No one told me how to behave as a young woman, so I watched how women acted on reality TV shows, movies, and social media. When I flashed my tits and ass, I thought that's what I was supposed to do.

No one told me that my personality should lead, so I watched how my friends, the women in my family and neighborhood, and the hair salons acted. So, I led with my body.

No one told me to respect my body, so when he asked me to send him naked pictures, I did. He sent it to all my classmates and posted them on social media, leaving me ashamed and humiliated.

No one told me that being a virgin was cool, so when the ugly boy from class asked me to come over to his house after school to have sex, I did it just so my friends wouldn't tease me about being a virgin or feel like I was the girl no one wanted to have sex with.

No one told me I was in control of my body, so when a boy demanded that we have sex without a condom, I didn't even have the voice to object. I simply allowed him unprotected access.

No one told me how to recognize the changes in my body or the odors it produced, so I didn't know that the foul smell coming from between my legs signaled that something wasn't right. So I waited until it itched and burned so badly before I went to a doctor and needed a shot to clear the disease that spawned in my body.

No one told me that my menstrual cycle was a time preserved for my body to naturally undergo its shedding process and should do so uninterrupted, so when he persuaded me, I allowed him to enter me during my sacred time.

No one told me that it was okay to say no — that I did not have to share my body, so I gave my body away time and time again.

No one told me that I would be wanted only for my pussy, so I believed every boy that told me they wanted a relationship with me, only to find myself crying each time he disappeared after we had sex a couple of times.

No one told me I was cute, so I was left always feeling unwanted and undesirable. So, when the first boy who told me I was cute asked me to suck his dick and his friends' dicks, I was happy to do it because he made me feel wanted.

No one told me I was beautiful, so when a boy told me that for the first time, I gave away my power and my body to him and three of his friends to later find myself 15 and pregnant with no idea who the father was.

No one told me how to value myself and that I should value myself, so I didn't understand my worth or the worth I should have.

Now, I'm a 16-year-old mother with the responsibility of raising a daughter. What do I tell her? Because no one told me, I made mistakes that could have been avoided.

I guess I will tell her everything I lived through in hopes she won't make the same mistakes. Because no one told me, I learned the hard way. I do not want the same for her.

No one told me, but I believe it's time to stop the cycle!

CHAPTER THREE

YOU ARE MORE THAN PUSSY

Women, you are precious! You are a beautiful human being. Your life is precious, and you possess a particularly precious jewel: your pussy! However, your body and your pussy can never be more precious than your life. Your value is not and should not be rooted in your pussy. Your pussy should not control your self-esteem. You have far more to offer. Never devalue yourself.

Ladies, you need to know!

You are more than pussy!

What is a woman? We are mothers, sisters, friends, creators, nurturers, warriors, pioneers, and so much more. Women have fought and continue to fight for equal treatment and equal rights and move beyond the shadows of their predecessors. Women continue to forge forward and show their intelligence, ambition, drive, competence, and skills as not only women but human beings. We are far more than the stereotypes devised by society to keep us silent and subservient. Yet, in a time when women are crying to be seen, heard, counted, respected, to have a seat at the table, and hold prominent positions, each step forward is countered by women posting pictures on social media in bikinis, half-naked, or nothing at all. And while it seems that seeing such pictures are becoming normalized, for them to continue to maintain their shock value, they must be more provocative than the last. It is particularly disheartening because is this really how you want the world, never mind the media, to perceive you?

While many of us strive to change the image and perspective of women valued for nothing more than our womb, body, or sex, there is a subversive element undermining our efforts. They are everywhere — ass and tit pictures, bikini, and soft porn pictures that were unthinkable even a few years ago. Is it such a desperate craving for attention or belief that you cannot be seen as attractive without showing your body? Do you think that your worth is tied only to your body or physical appearance? Do you feel you offer nothing more? How disturbing is it to see women strive for more shock value with each posting merely to prove that they have something marketable to use as a commodity?

Isn't your self-esteem more important than hordes of mindless followers? There was a time when women dressed modestly but were still considered classy, attractive, and sexy. Today, it seems that women feel that wearing less is the only way to validate their worth and attractiveness.

Why? What have we become? Aren't you tired of being considered as nothing more than sex, a body, tits, ass, an object? Why should your self-esteem be connected to your body, ass, or pussy? Yes, the human body is a beautiful piece of art, and yes, when you feel like you have a beautiful body, you want to flaunt it. However, isn't there a proper time and place for that? Why allow yourself to be reduced to an amateur porn star by flaunting your body? Are you a product? Is your pussy an item in a shopping cart? We want people to take us seriously, respect us, and appreciate us as women for more than pussy, but then we tease, taunt, and tempt with our pussy and cry when that's all someone wants from us! Let's call it what it is. Bikini pictures and tits and ass shots are essentially amateur porn. Just because you aren't getting paid for it doesn't make it any more excusable. Why the need to exploit your body? Is that what ultimately defines us? Pussy is part of us, but it should not lead or define who we are as women.

Maybe there is something to cultures where women cover up. And while some would consider that extreme, we have to ask how we can consider ourselves classy, elegant women when we feel that our attraction to someone must start with advertising or showcasing our bodies? Sure, attraction is initially everything, but if you think the key to attracting someone is advertising your body like products on a store shelf and not leaving anything to the imagination, then you don't believe you have anything to offer or that the best of you is only what you have between your legs. At some point, you have to learn to love yourself enough to move beyond simply being Pussy.

You are more than your pussy! Stop leading with your ass! Stop leading with your tits! Stop leading with your pussy! Don't you have more to offer? When you lead only with the "marketable" parts of your body, you cannot expect people to consider you as more than a body!

You bring more to the table than your body, than sex, than pussy! Why are you shaking your naked ass on social media for all to see? What is the purpose? What is your goal? What are you advertising? Certainly not your brain! Is your ass all you have to offer? Are you looking for validation? If you know you have a nice ass, why do you need to post it for views, likes, or hearts? Stop looking to others to bolster your self-esteem! When you depend on others to boost your self-esteem, you surrender control to those people. You allow them to persuade and influence you, particularly if they know you are vulnerable to compliments, and thereby place yourself in an unsafe situation. I ask again, what is your intention? If all you think you are doing, or if you convince yourself that you are simply showing off your "beautiful ass", you are essentially advertising pussy. I'm not saying you cannot wear sexy clothes. What I'm saying is that revealing your body can be done with class and elegance.

You are so much more than pussy! Pussy should not own or define you. You own and define your pussy! No matter what anyone does or does not tell you, you are beautiful and unique in your own way! There is no set definition of beauty, so don't let someone hold you to their eyes of beauty. Only you can believe in your beauty. Forget about what you see on TV shows, magazines, and social media. It's nothing more than smoke and mirrors reflecting a manufactured stereotype of beauty. But who gives others the right to define you? You should not follow those standards because they don't work! The very women you admire and think are beautiful compared to you are the same women who others cheat on, mistreat, and are considered as nothing more than pussy! They don't escape abuse or mistreatment, so you see, beauty is not just about looks, it's what you have and believe is beauty. However, this belief should never be based on your pussy! If pussy is the only thing you feel makes you worthy, then you need to take a long, hard look at your self-esteem and ask yourself why you feel this way.

You are more than pussy! Stop leading with it. If you want someone to want you for more than your pussy, stop leading with it! You must move beyond pussy because you have more to offer, and pussy will never sustain a relationship. You are not an object or toy. You are a woman with the most beautiful qualities. Do you recognize them? If someone asked you what they are, would you shake your tits in their face and say, "the girls"? Do you even recognize your qualities? Think about how you would define yourself. Not by what you do, what you wear, how big your ass is, how big your tits are, how good you make someone feel. It's none of those things! But who are you as a person! Think about that for a moment. If you cannot communicate or articulate your worth beyond your body, you need to take a step back and think about who you are and who you want to be.

Your pussy is not your value or self-esteem! Your self-esteem is rooted in self-respect for yourself and your body! Your self-esteem is your belief in your self-worth, not how someone else defines you. Only you have the power to put a value on yourself, and you are worth so much more than you give yourself credit for. Your self-esteem comprises all your qualities beyond the physical — it's your personality, intelligence, kindness, sense of humor, and the very uniqueness that distinguishes you from every other woman in the world! Be this unique woman you were destined to be and cherish your beauty, and more importantly, your self-love. You are more than pussy! You have so much more to offer than your body, sex, or your pussy! You just have to believe it!

You are more than pussy! Do not allow people to use you or treat you as nothing more than a sexual plaything. You are not a booty call! Do not use your body to get someone to like you, be with you, or stay with you. Do not use your body as a bargaining tool to get someone to see you as worthy! Never allow people to mistreat you, abuse you, or traffic you for your body! It's important for you to understand that you are more than pussy because there are dangerous predators who will see you as nothing more than a commodity to be bought and sold for the pleasure of others. It is critically important for you to understand that you must always protect yourself, find your voice, and speak out against anyone who seeks to harvest you for your pussy! Do not allow that to happen! No is not a bad word, but it is an underutilized word that I strongly suggest you use as a weapon. NO, you will not be considered invisible, used, mistreated, hurt, or disrespected. You will yell, NO! You have the power. You just have to use the power within you. You know you deserve better.

You are a human being, a precious human being that deserves to be treated with love, respect, and admiration. That all starts with you! Love and respect yourself enough so that you don't have to lead with pussy. You are so much more!

You are more than pussy, so let's move beyond pussy!

CHAPTER FOUR

YOUR PUSSY, YOUR PLEASURE

Your pussy is crying for satisfaction! Your body is crying for satisfaction! You deserve satisfaction! Stop being the one-stop-pleasing shop for someone else. You are a sexual being with needs, wants, and desires. Stop cheating the pussy and begin to please your pussy!

Ladies, you need to know!

Your pussy, your pleasure!

Many women have never experienced an orgasm. However, the same certainly does not appear to apply to men. Men seem to reach the finish line almost every time, while most women are left secretly wanting to cum and to experience the intense orgasm that men do during sex or intimacy. However, far too often, women are left unsatisfied after sex or intimacy because they are afraid to tell their partners what they like, need, and what they are missing to be sexually fulfilled or satisfied. Many would rather fake an orgasm than tell their partner that they missed the mark. When you fake an orgasm, you are being untrue to yourself and your partner. Why work hard to please your partner but not yourself as well?

What is it about women feeling embarrassed or uncomfortable about telling their sexual partners what they need for their pleasure? Interestingly, while women are afraid to tell their partner what to do and how to do it, they are unafraid to share their most prized possession — their body. And such fear leaves too many women disappointed, unfulfilled, unsatisfied, and sexually frustrated because they are afraid to say lick here, touch here, stay right there, rub this, bite this, flick this, slap that, turn me over, change positions, talk to me, and anything else that makes them feel good. Instead, we make it all about our partners and less about us and essentially fake orgasm and lie about our enjoyment. Stop, stop, stop cheating yourself! Stop cheating your pussy! It's your pussy, your pleasure!

Your throbbing pussy urges you to fulfill YOUR sexual needs! It does not throb to tell you to satisfy someone else's. Will you admit that you are a sexual being? That you get turned on, sexually excited, sexually aroused, and need some sexual healing? That you may not have blue balls, but at times, you have aching walls and a pulsating pussy? That your walls are throbbing so much that it awakens and distracts you to the point that you have to do something to calm it down. That jumping jacks, exercise, or not trying to think about it simply does not work. It needs attention, sexual healing. It needs a shot of pleasure! The need, desire, and throbbing become so intense, it's like a boiling tea kettle that starts to whistle from built-up pressure.

Well, your throbbing pussy is that kettle. The juices need to flow, and there's only one solution, but the last thing you want is to give yourself to someone who cannot please you until you erupt with pure satisfaction. Why? Because simply having sex with someone who is only focused on their satisfaction leaves you unfulfilled, angry, and disappointed. Even worse, it leaves you with an angry pussy that has not uttered a single whistle! But we have no one to blame but ourselves if we refuse to speak up about our needs! We cannot be more concerned about hurting someone's feelings if we tell them they are not pleasing us than we are about ensuring our own pleasure. Maybe your partner is waiting for you to instruct them on how to please you?

Or could it be that women do not know what they like, which is why they cannot communicate to their partner what they need to orgasm. Are we afraid to say it out loud? Are we uncomfortable talking about sex, pleasure, and our sexual desires? If so, you will always cheat yourself of pleasure! You cannot experience the full pleasure of sex or intimacy, and you surely will never please your pussy! After all, every woman is unique. It's not a one-performance-fits-all scenario. Everyone has different desires and needs. Partners exploring each other's sexual zones and pleasure points is fun, but communicating your individual pleasure can get you there faster.

Do you know what makes you feel good? Have you explored your body to discover what makes you feel good?

Have we failed or fear exploring our bodies to discover what makes us feel good? Could it be all the taboo teachings, miscommunications, and falsehoods we have grown to believe? That it is not okay to speak about our bodies, touch, or explore them, and that it is only for someone else's pleasure and to produce children, but not OUR pleasure? Could it be that we allowed others to tell us what our bodies should or should not like? Have we surrendered our pleasure to the control of others instead of taking control of our bodies, needs, and pleasures?

It is time to explore your body. Stop playing around with your pussy and start to play with your pussy! Get comfortable with your body. Do you even know what your body looks like? Do you know what your pussy looks like? Have you ever stood naked in front of a mirror and admired your body? If not, why not? If you do not admire yourself, admire your body, appreciate who you are, then how do you expect someone else to admire you? You are beautiful, flaws and all, love handles and all, so embrace the unique beauty that is your body! Learn what touch it takes to bring your body pleasure because before you can please the pussy, you must get to know your body!

Your pussy, your pleasure!

Look at your pussy. Touch it, feel it. You need to know what it looks like. Could you identify your pussy if you had to? You need to familiarize yourself with it. Take a mirror, spread your legs, and look at your pussy! Open it, touch it, feel it. Touch the lips, the clitoris. Let your fingers explore. Rub, massage, and play with it. Discover what it likes and which touch turned you on. Did you bring yourself to orgasm? Did you make a mental note of what made you feel good?

Now, touch your body and your breasts. Grab, pinch, and do whatever it takes to feel pleasure. Touch your arms, legs, stomach, face, and neck. Touch everywhere. Touch your pussy and other parts of your body simultaneously. Explore, explore, explore! What touch in combination with others fueled your pleasure? Again, make a mental note or even physical notes, and show them to your partner if you are hesitant to express what makes you feel good.

After exploring your pussy and body with your hands, consider exploring with toys, objects such as vibrators and nipple teasers, feather tickler, the feeling of leather whip straps brushing across your body, or even some clitoral/clit sensitizer/arousal gel. Just explore and free yourself sexually. Your pussy is waiting with bated breath to explode with joy, but only you can create and learn from the experience. If you don't know the geography of your pussy, you will not enjoy what others enjoy from it. You will only cheat yourself. If someone else so desires the pleasure the pussy brings to them, it is important to understand what pleasures your pussy provides to you!

Once you discover what makes you feel good, you will have a choice. You can either tell your partner what you like, what turns you on, and help guide them to please you or suffer in silence and frustration because once you know what it feels like to feel good, to be genuinely turned on, and what if feels like to experience an orgasm, you will want nothing less! I am not advocating masturbation, but if you do not know what it takes to get you there, then you cannot tell someone how to take you there! So please, do not leave the pussy crying. Leave the pussy satisfied.

Your pussy, your pleasure!

You are not exclusive to your pussy. You are inclusive and the master of your pussy! Your pussy is not solely for the pleasure of another. Your pussy should serve your needs and desires! Any intimacy or sexual intercourse should be a mutual decision not by force, capture, abuse, or sale! Sex is an experience meant to be shared, not one that leaves you curled up on the bed angry and dissatisfied. Don't let that happen! That should never happen! You must open your mouth for more than servicing someone else! Open your mouth to tell your partner what you need, want, and like so you can experience a wonderful orgasm and your pussy is satisfied and flowing with juice!

Speak up and tell your partner how you like it. Instruct your partner. They should want to please you and learn what you like. After all, they certainly know what they like and will make sure they have an orgasm. To end a sexual encounter without an orgasm is cheating your pussy! You and your pussy will be doing everything to please your partner, how about pleasing the pussy and more importantly, ending with your satisfaction? Again, I am confused why so many women are not afraid to share their body, surrender their pussy, let someone enter their body, and yet are afraid to speak up and tell their sexual partners what they like or do not like, and more importantly, what you will not allow!

Women, you are precious, your body is precious. If you can open yourself up, allow someone to insert their penis, their tongue, their fingers, toys, and/or objects into your pussy, then you should have no problem telling someone what you like and need them to do to achieve pleasure and fulfillment. Stop faking! Talk to your partner during sex and tell them a little to the left, a little to the right, slower, faster, harder, softer, bite, grip, touch, rub, yes, stay right there! Also, tell them when you are on the brink of cumming and again once you have cum. Communicating your pleasure point could be a turn-on for them knowing that they pleased you! Don't you want something more from sex than pleasing your partner? What about your pleasure or satisfaction? I know your pussy wants more and does not want to feel like it is only a servant.

Your pussy, your pleasure!

Stop playing with the pussy! Stop cheating the pussy! Stop being someone else's pleasure by allowing only them to enjoy your pussy. Your pussy is for your pleasure first! Sexual healing is good for the mind and body. An orgasm can leave you shivering with pleasure. Don't you want to end your sexual experiences tingling from head to toe?

Women, we give so much of ourselves. How about some sexual gratification and pleasure for us?

Remember, your pussy, your pleasure. You control the benefits!

CHAPTER FIVE

PUSSY CHASERS, HUNTERS, AND MOLESTERS

There are always those who will pursue pussy for one reason or another, some for their own selfish need and pleasure and others for personal gain and profit. Either way, predators are a real and dangerous threat that can severely impact or even threaten your safety and life. Beware!

Ladies, you need to know!

There are pussy predators out there, and you need to be vigilant.

The pleasure of pussy is like a drug to those who need it, crave it, and market it. It is an addiction as serious as any substance or alcohol abuse and produces a high that will drive those who crave it to any lengths to obtain it. For women and girls around the world, it is an asset that is abused, bought, and sold like any other commodity. But we are not products. We are not objects or playthings, but human beings with the right to control and protect our bodies and pussies.

In the '80s, the crack epidemic was at its peak. Users would do anything and use anyone to get enough money to feed their habit. The same applies to those who need to use pussy, but there has never been a season or peak for this epidemic. Unfortunately, this is one epidemic without a cure.

The grim reality is that people will do whatever it takes to claim that sweet sticky thing between your legs.

You must be vigilant and learn to identify the nature of pussy prowlers. There are three types: Chasers, Hunters, and Molesters. Chasers hunt for pussy solely to satisfy their selfish needs and pleasure. They love pussy, cannot get enough pussy, and crave it from as many women or girls as they can get. They love the game of it all and collect pussy like they collect sports trophies to display in a cabinet. They want their phones filled with the phone numbers of their "trophies" and always have their eye out for the next conquest.

Chasers see you as nothing more than sex, a tool to use to fulfill their sexual desires and needs. Sure, some will care about you, some will pretend to care about you, and some will make it clear that they want nothing more than a hookup. Chasers are scheming, devious, and sexually voracious. They are obsessed with pussy and how to get more! While many believe they are not out to intentionally harm a woman, their behavior is riddled with lies and deception that only causes heartache, pain, and often, worse consequences. When someone is focused only on their needs and acts accordingly, there can only be one winner in such a relationship. Chasers become users, manipulators, and it is typically the woman who ends up victimized by such destructive and selfish behavior. Honesty and compassion are nowhere to be found in the empty souls of Chasers. Women are merely points on a scorecard.

Chasers view your feelings and needs as alien worlds they have no desire to explore. Anything beyond your body, your pussy, presents no challenge or interest to them. After all, they have what they need. They get so excited about pussy that they try to help their family and friends get pussy too even if it means sharing a woman at the same time. They will try to persuade, manipulate, and convince the woman they are involved with to have group sex. This is dangerous for women, especially if they have no desire to engage in sexual activities with more than one person. While some women enjoy threesomes, foursomes, and group sex, participants should be willing and not bullied, coerced, or threatened into participating to please or be considered loyal to a Chaser. Such activity can be considered rape or sex trafficking. But Chasers see it as nothing more than harmless sex that a woman should be willing to engage in. Do not fall for this! If you have to be forced, coerced, or bullied, this is not harmless!

Then you have pussy Hunters. They want pussy not for themselves but for others. They want pussy to place on sale. Hunters are conniving, manipulative, and calculating predators that will do anything to claim your pussy and to claim you! They carefully plan how to lure and trap you either alone or with the help of others to sell you and your pussy for their profit. These are pimps, sex traffickers, and yes, your partner or significant other. People who will persuade you to sell your pussy for their profit along with those who will enslave you, control you, and ship you around the world to sell your pussy to the highest bidder. They will drug you, beat you, abuse you, and make you do unthinkable things as if you were nothing more than a mindless doll. Your humanity means nothing to them. It is simply an obstacle to be removed in their efforts to lure you into their trap. They will lie, compliment, charm, and deceive you. They carefully stalk their unsuspecting prey like serpents slithering through the grass. All they want and care about is your pussy! You must be aware! Your life depends on it!

Lastly, you have Molesters who lurk in an ever lower, baser category. They exist merely to corrupt innocence for their own pleasure and take advantage of the vulnerable and snatch away their childhood, adolescence, and even adulthood. These master manipulators easily transfer guilt to their victims and are often disguised as a loving friend who pretends to care about you but becomes a puppet master pulling the strings of coercion and perversion. Subtly and not so subtly, they envelop their victims in a web so tightly spun that there is only command and obey under threat of violence or harm.

The most terrifying reality is that the faces of Chasers, Hunters, and Molesters use to be considered strangers, but that is a myth. These predators are not lurking on distant shores but in our relationships, workplaces, families, and communities. So many believe that it cannot happen in their own backyards, but these cases are the most common because these issues are often ignored and disregarded. Predators look like our partners, friends, families, co-workers, supervisors, coaches, teachers, neighbors, and people you interact with daily — above all, people you trust. Be careful of those who want you to sit on their lap, who always want to hug you, kiss you, compliment you on how you are becoming a woman or how beautiful you look. Always speak out if someone says something that makes you uncomfortable, if they are doing something that does not feel right, or if they are touching you inappropriately. Be mindful of people you frequently associate with or are empowered to take advantage of you because of their position in your life. No one is exempt, and you must be aware!

If you are a female of any age, it is important for you to love yourself and recognize your beauty, value, and how to determine right from wrong. No one deserves to be forced to do anything against their will, particularly if it does not feel right. It's never permissible for anyone to touch you inappropriately! You are precious. Your body is precious. You must protect yourself and your pussy! You are worthy of so much more and deserving of so much more!

Feeling unworthy, ugly, and needing to validate your beauty are the signs predators look for. They prey on your weaknesses and insecurities by flattering and complimenting you. While we all enjoy compliments, affirmation of your beauty is something only you can truly provide to yourself. You should not need others to tell you. For example, has someone ever complimented you on your hair, clothing, or makeup? Yes, you should appreciate a genuine compliment, but it should merely confirm what you already know — that you look good! Stop relying on others to validate you.

Most importantly, be vigilant of those who over-compliment you. I am not talking about genuine compliments, but those showered on you by others who use flattery as a tool to manipulate and maneuver you by telling you that you are so beautiful you could be a model or actress. Sure, you could be a model or actress, but please do not be fooled by the model/actress scout game. This is usually followed by a request to meet somewhere for a modeling or casting call or to take pictures. Not that you are not beautiful enough to be an actress or model (neither of which are solely based on looks), but again, do not be fooled. Legitimate scouts or agencies do not work this way, nor do they ask to meet you alone. This is a trap, regardless of whether it is a man or woman. If they are legitimate, they will have no problem meeting you in a public place or their office, preferably with a friend or family member present. Always ask for their credentials. Think of it as a date, and let someone know where you are going and who you are meeting. Do not allow yourself to become a victim by being abducted, raped, drugged, and prostituted for trusting someone else more than your own instincts! Trust yourself above anyone else at all times!

Social media is another playground for predators. Do not be fooled or swayed by profiles because people can easily hide behind lies and fake photos. Dating sites, in particular, are a perfect example of this. The internet is notorious for scams and predators lurking in the shadows. It can be almost impossible to verify someone's identity short of running a background check, yet many women still become victims. I cannot stress this strongly enough. Never meet anyone alone, at night, in an unfamiliar, or remote area. Would you let a child do this? So then why would you put yourself at the same risk?

But there are more devious ways to lure and entrap that do not even require a physical meeting. If someone asks you to send nude or compromising photos, refuse! Block them. Report them. Delete them. Those photos can easily end up in the wrong hands and shared in ways that can cause serious harm at work, school, relationships, and your safety.

If someone pressures or coerces you into doing something that makes you uncomfortable, trust your instincts. For example, if someone tries to touch you, feel you, take off your clothes, or force themselves on you, scream, yell, shout, say NO! If it feels wrong, your instincts already know that it is wrong. Listen to your instincts. Listen to the voice in your head. Never ignore these warnings! They exist for a reason. If you cannot risk speaking, write, text, carve it on a wall, leave clues, do what you can to safely bring attention to yourself.

Unfortunately, it is extremely easy for predators to hide. One reason is that they seldom look like monsters. Their faces are recognizable to us as people we know, love, and trust. If someone threatening approached you, you would not think twice about avoiding them. The same should apply to "normal" people. Just because they may not look like predators does not mean that they may not be one. Your best defense is you, your attitude, your vigilance.

Question everything. Question everyone! Be wary of anyone who wants to connect with you. Do not be fooled by sugary compliments, smooth talk, or too-good-to-be-true promises, lifestyles, or representations. When you learned to walk, you learned one step at a time. Sometimes you stumbled. Sometimes you fell. But you were determined, so you kept trying until you walked and finally ran. Apply the same technique to the people in your life and those who come into your life because interaction with others is like learning to walk. You have to focus on your balance, on taking steady steps, and not falling. You learn from your mistakes and become confident enough to sprint.

Pussy is considered the antidote, the cure, the answer to satisfying sexual needs, fetishes, and fantasies. It is also a commodity as valuable as gold and a magnet to those who seek to use it for profit. Unfortunately, predators are all around us smiling behind faces we love and trust as well as in the friendliness of strangers or people coming into our lives. Claim the power of your pussy by not allowing yourself to become a victim or the next statistic. Your pussy should be your power, not your weakness or vulnerability.

CHAPTER SIX

CARE FOR YOUR PUSSY

How you care for your pussy is all about how you view yourself.

Ladies, you need to know!

You must care for your pussy.

The greatest gift you can give yourself is the gift of self-care, self-love, and self-respect. Your beliefs, perspective, and knowledge about your body and pussy will shape your decisions, actions, speech, and outlook. The way you honor and respect yourself will determine how well you care for yourself.

As a female, it is critically important for you to understand and/or adopt a mantra of respect, protection, love, and hygiene, which encapsulates your well-being and preciousness as a human being. When we think about something precious, we think about how treasured, valuable, and cherished it is. Do you know that a precious gem is considered precious because it is rare, beautiful, and valuable? Then this should also be how you define yourself.

As a precious gem, you must take care of yourself. It starts with respecting your body. Our body is our life. How we take care of our body includes what we put into it, how we treat and protect it, and how we love it. Never take life for granted because it is so important, and you must do everything to sustain it. You must put yourself first! First means choices and behavior based on what's best for you rather than what you want or what others want from you. Respect your body!

When we think about what we put into our bodies, we think about what we eat, drink, or medications we take. However, we also have to consider other things that enter our body, particularly our pussy! From a nutrition and life-balance perspective, we must be mindful of everything affecting our bodies. However, we must also be mindful of what we allow to enter our pussy, be it a penis, tongue, toys, or other things. What enters our body in any way must be considered with care and caution. Remember, you are a gem!

Therefore, treat yourself like a priceless gem and control access to your pussy! To share your pussy is to share you! Everyone does not have the right to have you because you are precious!

Do you know what is even more precious? Virginity. Many times, virgins are made to feel guilty for not having sex or sharing their body. But being a virgin is a good thing because this means you are untouched and at your purest — the rarest gem of all. This is something to be proud of because you do not have to worry about the potential problems and complications sex can bring. As a virgin, you have something so special that many would stop at nothing to be your first sexual experience, but others will try to steal it from you any way they can. Instead of respecting this treasure, you become a commodity for those who want it at any cost. But remember who controls your body. You! And therefore, you control your pussy. You should be proud of your virginity. It's nothing to make fun of or ridicule. It's something that you maintain as a choice. It's the power to control your own body and decide when and with whom to share this precious gift. In an era when everything is sexualized to the point of cheapness and fleeting gratification, you should applaud yourself for holding yourself to a higher value than a series of meaningless encounters.

Whether you are a virgin or not, your preciousness is the attitude and behavior you must adopt regarding your body. As a female, you must learn how to physically care for your body and pussy. Do you practice good hygiene? Do you take frequent showers or spend time soaking in the bathtub? Do you pay attention to your teeth, nails, hair, feet, and skin? Good personal hygiene is essential! Ensure that your pussy is clean and fresh at all times. There is an unfortunate belief that unclean pussy smells fishy, but good hygiene plays an important part in controlling odor.

Females also produce a natural cleaning discharge and pH. However, your pH can be easily affected by using certain products. It's important to be cautious about using douches, feminine sprays, and certain bath products and soaps that may affect your pH balance. Pay attention if a discharge looks or smells unusual, or if you notice itching, burning, or irritation, take immediate action. It could be something as simple as a yeast infection caused by a product or dietary issue, but it could also be something more serious like a sexually transmitted disease. This is why it is so critical to be attuned to your body.

Some sexually transmitted diseases like syphilis, gonorrhea, and chlamydia can be treated, but others like herpes and HIV/AIDS can last a lifetime. That's why it's important to be selective about sharing your body to avoid consequences, whether it's vaginally, orally, or anally. Sharing your body can expose yourself to infection and disease, which is why you must think with your head instead of your heart to protect your pussy, body, and life!

In addition to paying attention to your body's needs, there is a particularly sensitive time when you should be even more attentive — during your menstrual period — your body's natural monthly cleansing. It is especially critical to stay fresh and clean during your monthly period because bleeding can create unpleasant odors. Change your tampon or pad frequently and bathe daily. Also, during your monthly period, you should allow your body time to do what it needs to do. When a computer is scheduled for maintenance, certain functions cannot be performed during that time. The same should apply to your monthly period. Allow your vagina to function as it is meant to without interruption. Many may try to persuade you that this is the perfect time to have sex because you cannot get pregnant, but that is not true. There is still a small chance depending on when you ovulate. You can also still contract a disease, so take control of your body and allow your vagina to do what it must. Intimacy does not have to always be about intercourse. It can be so much more. Respect your body, and your body will respect you!

If you have decided to be sexually active, valuing yourself should include getting to know the person you plan to share your body with. You must become comfortable with yourself and with asking questions because it is critical to your safety, health, and control. Learning to communicate before having sex is critical to your well-being. Ask questions before sharing your body and pussy. Know who you are dealing with and make expectations and limitations clear!

That's why it's so important to know who you are before sharing yourself with someone else. Too often, women suffering from body insecurities feel uncomfortable having a partner look at their bodies, therefore they are uncomfortable looking at their partner's body. This is a huge mistake. Eagerness and impatience to have sex often mean not examining your partner and reaching for protection — a big NO! I'm not trying to kill spontaneity because that's an important and exciting element to sex, but what's more important is your well-being and safety. Get to know your partner's body. Examine their genitals, check for anything unusual, and note any unpleasant odors. If you've ever ordered a pizza, when it arrives, you open the box to check it. If it has mold on the sauce or smells off, would you eat it? The same mindset should apply to your partner. Always remember that your health and life depend on your decisions. If your partner values you, they should not object to this, and you can even incorporate it into foreplay. Take notice if they are reluctant or unwilling. If they are hiding something, it now becomes your responsibility to protect yourself and not their ego, secrets, or ulterior motives.

Ask your partner about their sexual orientation, if they are disease-free, or have any other sexual issues or concerns. Explain what you are comfortable doing, not doing, have never tried, or are open to. Information empowers you to make safe and sound decisions before becoming sexually involved with someone. Never surrender your power or choices! Remember, your life, your body, your pussy, your decisions, your control!

If you are uncomfortable with who you are, your body, or honest talk with your sexual partner, you may not be ready for sexual activity or intimacy!

Whether you maintain your virginity, have had sex but have decided to abstain, or are sexually active, you must do everything you can to protect yourself. That means always putting yourself first!

How you nurture and care for yourself mirrors how you feel about yourself. You are precious, beautiful, and priceless.

Treat yourself like the gem you are!

CHAPTER SEVEN

THE POWER OF YOUR VOICE

Your voice, your power, use it!

Ladies, you need to know!

The power of your voice.

Speak up, speak out, speak boldly! Your voice is your superpower — use it for good, to protect yourself, to care for yourself, to shine the light on wrong, and more importantly, use it to communicate YOUR wants, desires, and objections.

Your voice is the most powerful tool you have to combat anything that threatens you. Your voice is the kryptonite to anyone who would harm you. But you must learn to use it. Not fear it. Not hide from it. Not question it. But use it to shout to the world that you are here.

Your voice matters. For far too long, women were expected to sit silently in the shadows, mute and invisible to the world. Many cultures still adhere to this outdated practice and treat women as little more than commodities. Yet consider what the world would be like without women. Could men survive? Of course not! It cannot always be about men. Women are the givers and nurturers of life of all kinds. We were never meant to be objects, subordinates, or slaves. You have only to look at the contributions women have made throughout history to understand what we have accomplished. So imagine if women everywhere had the same opportunities and freedom to excel in whatever they chose rather than be treated like cattle. Imagine how much more advanced the world would be if every girl who dreamed of becoming a doctor, scientist, engineer, artist, or whatever she wanted, was allowed the simple privilege of doing so without antiquated social stigma, opposition, or even violence. Imagine if women had a unified voice. Imagine if women used their *voice.*

Such archaic attitudes and mindsets are no longer acceptable! Some are based on faith or religious beliefs, but while I am not diminishing the importance of following one's faith, women can still be proud, fierce, and follow their faith. We will be seen. We will be heard. And we will express ourselves. Many will attempt to demean or dismiss the importance of what you have to say. They will complain that a woman's place is not to speak up, but to remain silent and subservient. Of course, we have our roles as mothers, wives, daughters, and nurturers. But this does not dismiss our worthiness as women, as human beings. This does not give the right to anyone to silence you. You are not inferior, and your voice is as strong as your beliefs that are borne from your confidence and determination as a woman.

Communication is essential to your life and well-being. The ability to exchange information, express yourself, your feelings and emotions, and engage in conversation is critical to your ability to protect yourself, your body, and your pussy. What you say and how you say it is critical in protecting yourself but also reveals how you regard yourself. It reflects your self-confidence. It is a mirror to your personality. Use that mirror to show the world that you are not invisible. That you will not remain in the shadows.

Use your voice to speak positively about yourself. Never disrespect yourself by calling yourself derogatory names like bitch. How is this an acceptable term for yourself? A bitch is a female dog. Are you a dog? Is this how you want the world to regard you? It is not a term of endearment, but a term of derision! Don't fall into that trap. Social media and music should not dictate your perception of yourself. So why should you lower your value by labeling yourself as an animal? You should not follow but take the lead, change the conversation, and change your speech to represent who you are and how you view yourself! If you refer to yourself negatively or put yourself down, this will signal to others that it is acceptable to do so. They will become comfortable in viewing you as something inferior because this is the impression you gave them. Refer to yourself with affirming and positive words and expressions. If you only talk about your pussy, you will be seen as nothing more than pussy. They will not see your face. They will not hear your words. Your pussy and sex should not be considered assets because you only devalue yourself if you believe this is all you have to offer. Not speaking out only reinforces stereotypes that have controlled women throughout time. And those who continue to adhere to these stereotypes make it that much more important for you to find your voice and use it. Change can only happen if enough voices are heard. Think about the women who fought for the right to vote. Think about the other women who championed causes, from equal pay to the right to birth control. Silence is never golden when it affects your life, safety, and freedom.

How you communicate will affect every part of your life and every relationship. Good communication is the lifeblood of every relationship and the connection between two people, but the inability to speak openly and honestly has destroyed countless relationships. If you cannot speak about your feelings, emotions, or concerns, or if your partner does not want to listen or acknowledge you, do not retreat into silence. Do not let such situations silence your voice. It can harm you in so many ways, including physical danger.

If you feel uncomfortable about a situation, speak up. Speak up about your choices, needs, concerns, desires, and beliefs. Never let anyone stifle your voice. Otherwise, you are handing them control over you. It may be subtle at first, but the more you remain silent, the more power you give to someone else. Your feelings are as powerful as your words or actions.

Communication regarding your pussy is also critical. You should be able to confidently tell someone no, that you are uncomfortable, or to leave you alone. Speak confidently and make your feelings known. Without communication, you put yourself in danger. When you fail to express yourself, ask questions, or respond in situations, you surrender control. Think of those old horror movies where the female character is in danger and running away, but always trips and falls. Is this stereotype of weakness what you want to embrace? That we are nothing more than victims who cannot defend ourselves? We have the power to change these negative perceptions by speaking out and making ourselves heard!

Your voice is powerful. It can be a tool, a weapon, or a conduit to change. You can gain help, support, and encouragement not only for yourself by speaking out, but for women everywhere.

Your voice, your power!

CHAPTER EIGHT
WHAT'S YOUR PUSSY'S NAME?

There's something to a name, and your pussy needs one!

Ladies, you need to know!

Your pussy needs a name!

If you have ever had the pleasure of hanging out with a group of women and talking about everything and anything, I bet the conversation turned to sex at some point. And it's during those conversations, with much laughter, that stories are shared about amazing sexual experiences, disappointments, partner ratings, sexual droughts, needs, or even sharing tips or techniques on how to please your partner or indulge in fantasies. It's all good fun and laughs.

And, if you ever engaged in such conversations, I'm sure you either heard some women talk, or maybe you were the woman who talked about your pussy's name. Yes, the name of your pussy, much the way you would name a pet. But not those old kitty cat or coo-coo nicknames. Those are childish and not deserving of a woman. I'm talking about the name you choose to call your pussy instead of simply saying, "pussy". After all, there is something about a name.

More often than not, you will find that woman and girls have actually named their pussy. Why not? Men have proudly created a cult about the names they call their penis.

They certainly have no inhibitions about it. But when it comes to naming your pussy, there's something far more personal about it, something liberating. There's something to a name — a single word! Think about it for a moment. The word "pussy" evokes strong feelings, reactions, and responses, some that can propel you to the heights of desire but also hurl you into danger and harm. A name truly holds more power than we ever imagined.

If you have not taken the time to name your pussy, do it! There is something so empowering about naming your pussy! It creates a connection and a bond that brings your relationship with your pussy to a different level. There's something to a name. I wonder if women who have named their pussy would agree that they have often used their pussy's name to seduce, entice, excite, and arouse their partner? A name not only makes it easier to talk about your pussy, but it can make sexual conversation more fun, honest, and comfortable. Using your pussy's name can release inhibitions and usher the confidence to speak more openly about sex, so there are definitely benefits to naming your pussy! But naming your pussy should not be exclusive to sexuality. It should resonate with you on a personal level because once named, your pussy is no longer anonymous. It will have a name, a personality, a presence. There is something to a name!

What if every female experienced a wonderful non-sexual reaction, connection, and awakening simply by naming their pussy? That naming their pussy brought meaning, responsibility, and accountability because a name created something more tangible than a body part?

If you already had a strong understanding and obligation to your pussy before naming it, can you imagine the stronger connection to your body and pussy? And for those who have not yet considered an appropriate name for their pussy, think about the awakening and bond they would experience because their pussy is no longer a separate entity. Your pussy was always part of your physical body, but now, it becomes an extension of you. There's something to a name.

A name bestows meaning, purpose, and life! A name acknowledges and recognizes a personal history. A name excites, commands, and demands. Names shock, offend, and disturb. But names can also endear, comfort, and soothe. They vocalize, assert, and make a statement to the world. It says, "I exist. I am here." Your pussy is here, and need you to recognize, acknowledge, and regard her with admiration.

I wonder that if women took the time to name their pussy, would they love it more? If named, would they care about it more? If named, would they guard it more?
If we named our pussy, would we treat it with more respect and caution? If we named our pussy, would we cherish and value it more? There's something to a name! Would we view our pussy as an extension of ourselves, of who we are, and as something precious and unique? Would we be more selective about sharing it?

LET'S TALK PUSSY | ALETHEA TAYLOR

You need to take your pussy seriously. There is something so endearing about taking the time to really think about the perfect name for your pussy. You give her a voice, a voice that hopefully causes you to stop, think, and consider everything related to her being. There's something to a name. Don't choose some random name without putting serious thought into it. Talk to your pussy, look at it, touch it, and do whatever you need to find inspiration for the perfect name for your pussy. How does she function, how does she secrete, how does she throb? Do you know the characteristics of your pussy? You should! Because if you took the time to get to know your pussy, you already know her characteristics and her personality. Have a conversation with her. You may be quite surprised as she just might lead you to the perfect name!

Name your pussy! Enjoy it. Savor it. After all, we are sexual beings and are entitled to fun and enjoyment too. If you take the time to name your pussy, you might see her as a miniature of yourself, which may be all you need to feel a stronger connection to your body, your pussy, and be aware that although she needs love and sexual satisfaction on your terms, above all, your pussy needs care and protection.

There's something to a name! What's your pussy's name?

CHAPTER NINE

PLEASE SEE ME

Please see me,

I am the innocent, sweet, and blind,

Blind to the belief that I can trust all kinds,

Kind to a fault to one and all,

All I see are God's amazing creations,

Creations of love, heart, and soul,

Soul I have, but to be sold without thought,

Thought that I am nothing but pussy and ass,

Ass for their pleasure, but none that is mine,

Mine is stolen from my precious body,

Body and feelings, I behold,

Behold nothing beyond heartless greed,

Greed for money and control,

Control me as if I am an animal,

An animal shackled, prodded, and abused,

Abused with no care for who I am,

I am precious. I answer, yes, you are,

Do you see me – yes, I do,

Are you listening – yes, I am,

LET'S TALK PUSSY | ALETHEA TAYLOR

Am I weak – no, you are strong,

Do you care – yes, I do,

Am I alone – no, you are not,

Can I speak – yes, please do,

But that's all in my head, the conversation I must have,

Have to keep my sanity or else I'll die,

Die at the hands of my captors because I am weary and
hopeless,

Hopeless maybe, but I find the strength to speak,

I scream out loud in hopes my words penetrate a mind,

I am your daughter, your sister, your niece, please treat me as
a sister, humankind,

Humankind is a connection we all share, but no one sees me,

I cannot understand why,

Why does my pussy mean so much to you that you cannot
see,

See that I am here, right in plain sight,

Sight to behold, sight to see, please see me, because you are
killing me for others to please.

CHAPTER TEN

CONSENT

Anything other than consent is a crime!

Ladies, you need to know!

If you do not give consent, then it is never okay regardless of the circumstances.

Attraction is almost like a dance. At first, it is slow and sensual, but as the heat builds up, as the flame ignites, the pace and rhythm increase. It starts with a look, a stare, the silent flirting that reveals itself in a smile, body language, the intensity of a stare. Then it transforms into assessment. We study the features, the hair, the clothing, and the movement the way we would admire a painting in a museum. Our bodies respond to the swag, the sexiness, and the charisma. Silent language becomes a voice, a remark, a compliment, all stepping stones that lead to conversation and wordplay. Chemistry and sexual attraction become primal magnets pulling two people together.

Now the dance becomes physical. Hands pull you into an embrace. Fingers, lips, and tongues become instruments in a sexual symphony. Arms embrace, legs entwine, eyes lock. Skin brushes against skin, and your bodies move and merge in passionate synchronicity. Then comes the exploration of different positions, the indulgence of fantasies, the introduction of toys and the playground of your imaginations, and maybe the journey into threesomes or group sex. Whatever music you move to, whatever desire fuels you, nothing happens without your consent!

No one gets to touch, kiss, feel, or do anything to get to your pussy without your consent! No one has the right to force, demand, or threaten you for sex or to have sex with others. It's your body. You alone control your body! Only you have the power of consent for your body and your pussy!

Consent is not given under threats, duress, or fear. Consent is not granted if you don't understand. Consent is not rendered because of bullying, coercion, or under the influence of drugs or alcohol. It is not consent if you are under the legal age of consent according to the laws of your state, and if you engage in sex with someone older than you, that could be considered statutory rape! If you do not agree to engage in sexual activity and it happens against your will, that is rape! If you give consent and begin to engage in sexual activity, but then decide that you do not want to continue, if you say stop, no, that you do not want to do it, or you push someone away because they disregard your wishes and force themselves on you, that is rape! Anything you say no to is not consent! It does not matter if you are in the heat of foreplay and decide not to continue. If you say no, everything should stop! If you are forced beyond your no, then that is sexual assault! You decide to give consent or denial of sexual activity.

Sexual excitement and arousal are natural. It's your body's response to attraction and a signal of sexual need. The excitement and feelings that ignite between two people often demand sexual satisfaction. It is easy to get caught in the thrill and passion of the moment, but regardless of the situation, action requires your consent! Sexual attraction should only proceed if it happens between two consenting individuals. However, such feelings are not always mutual. When someone wants sex with you and you do not share the same feelings, speak out! You are not a toy to be used just because someone else wants you. You decide who you want to share your body with, if at all.

No one controls your body or your pussy! They belong only to you. Your desires, needs, and wants are your decisions. Never surrender control no matter the argument or persuasion. Too many women allow themselves to be pressured, cajoled, or sweet-talked into sex. But this decision should be yours only when you are ready to engage in any type of sexual activity from flirting to foreplay, from oral sex to penetration, group sex, or anything sexually related. Your participation should only be what you feel comfortable with and what you agree to. It is all about the power of consent, and only you can give it!

Consent is power, a power that you control and should never surrender. Consent is your voice and your choice. The power of consent means complete control of your body at all times. Don't allow anyone to dictate what you should do with your body. Always keep control of your pussy. Make your consent clear. Make your objections clear. Silence is not golden. If anything, it is an invitation for abuse and control.

Anything other than consent is sexual assault, rape, or sex trafficking!

CONCLUSION

Women need to know. We all need to know!

Lives depend on knowledge and information!

Females around the world are being raped, molested, sexually assaulted, trafficked, and dying because we continue to either have sophomoric conversations about pussy, leave women and girls to struggle with little or incorrect information, or continue to fall prey to the word, "pussy". Someone, we, you, all of us, have an obligation to help a girl or woman because lives depend on it.

We must be willing to emerge from the shadows of stigma and embarrassment and be confident and bold enough to talk about pussy. Too many lives depend on our willingness to be stronger than a simple word. We must be unafraid to talk about it, unashamed to stand up, speak up, and speak out! We must find the courage to start conversations that prepare, encourage, and empower girls and women.

We must become comfortable with the word "pussy". Comfortable speaking it. Hearing it. Comfortable having educated conversations about pussy because the truth is, although we talk about pussy, we fail to educate about pussy. We must reclaim the power from the word to ultimately control the word so that women will take full control of their pussy.

There are some single mothers who do not know how to have a frank conversation about pussy with their daughters. There are some single fathers uncomfortable having this conversation with their daughters. Many couples don't know if or when they should have this conversation with their daughters or are too embarrassed to broach the subject. Meanwhile, females are deprived of the critical and life-saving information they need to know about their pussy. Teenage girls are headed to college but are unprepared for or unaware of the many dangers that may await them. Adult women are living in turmoil because they were not informed or encouraged to use their voices to speak up about what happened to them because of their pussy. Even as you read this, young girls and women are listening to others feed them misinformation about their pussy but believe what they are told because they are ill-equipped with the information they need to know about their pussy.

The unfortunate reality is that many of us cannot face or accept that countless girls and women remain ignorant of their own power or are socialized or indoctrinated not to question, speak, or challenge. Many are trained to be subservient, obedient, and dependent. Many are robbed or deprived of truth, education, or information they need to make informed decisions that start with knowledge about their pussy. How many of us have experienced the same challenges? How many of us were fortunate enough to have open discussions with family, friends, or others who could advise us honestly and without shame? Sex education in schools, if it even exists, is inadequate, and doesn't even begin to touch on the more widespread issues beyond pregnancy or sexually transmitted diseases. Even in today's world of technology and instant communication, there is a massive gap of critical understanding and knowledge.

There are interventions we can employ to decrease the victimization of girls and women around the world, but we must be willing to take action. We can no longer stand silent, stand afraid, or hope someone else will step in or step up and have that much-needed conversation about pussy. WE have to love, support, be honest, inform, prepare, and encourage girls and women. Caring can go a long way, but there must be a starting point.

The first lesson our girls learn about their body and their pussy should not come from the streets, misinformed men or women, or at the cost of rape, molestation, or trafficking. WE must find the courage and strength to talk to our girls. If we are too afraid to have an honest conversation, how can we expect our girls to muster the courage or find their voice to speak up, speak out, and speak boldly about their experiences? We must be willing to set an example and take responsibility for every female we know so they will be informed and also know that they can turn to and talk to us about anything because we care! The word "pussy" cannot hold us captive. Like it or not, the word echoes throughout the world, but it is only a word, and our concerns should not be squeamishness about it but saving lives. Saving girls and women from emotional and physical harm. If you saw someone attempting to cross the street against a red light, wouldn't you act? Consider the girls and women who face red lights because of their pussy. Would you choose to act or ignore the problem? We must be willing to act, talk, share, and support females. It is our obligation as human beings. Let our voices be heard so theirs won't be silenced! It's time to talk about pussy!

The word "pussy" is here to stay, and rape, molestation, and human trafficking cannot be ignored. If we are more worried about a word than we are about girls and women impacted by the day, the hour, or the minute because of their pussy, in some way, we bear responsibility for this situation. If we fail to educate, make aware, and prepare females of all ages everywhere about their pussy, then we are choosing to ignore them and leave them to a terrible fate that none deserve. We must teach them about their body and how to speak out. We must teach them how to say no and challenge anything that threatens their safety and well-being. We must help them learn that self-esteem and self-worth don't come from someone else, but that it's embedded within them. They need to know that searching for validation, acceptance, and love from others puts them in a dangerous and vulnerable situation to be used, abused, and dehumanized. Self-love comes from within and helping them understand and recognize that requires our help!

Our girls must learn to respect their bodies, use their voices, and find the confidence to stand strong and tall. But they cannot do that if they don't hear what they need, have support, or learn to walk in power — the power of information, of value, and to speak positively about themselves. It's about the power to recognize that they are more than pussy, that instead of shouting about their pussy or checking to receive a label of "good pussy", they understand that good pussy is cared for, protected, respected, and valued. Good pussy starts with how well they treat their pussy, not how someone else feels about it or wants to use it. The need to validate their pussy is a whistle call for those looking and listening for the opportunity to sell them, rape them, and mistreat them for their "good pussy".

Without our help, they may never understand how special and precious they are. Knowing that is important because how they consider themselves will make a huge difference in their lives. Sure, they will make mistakes, but maybe those mistakes will not bring devastating consequences because they were armed with the necessary information to make informed decisions.

Imagine how different things could be for women if they truly claimed and understood the nature and power of their pussy. Don't let your daughter, niece, sister, granddaughter, cousin, aunt, neighbor, student, or mentee walk out into the world without everything they need to know about their body and their pussy! They must be prepared and equipped to react to any situations they may encounter, be it at home, work, school, sports, traveling, or anywhere they go!

Knowledge is power. So, let's talk about pussy.

Lives depend on it!

ABOUT THE AUTHOR

Alethea Taylor is an entrepreneur, actor, and advocate for girls and women. She has built a credible reputation as a dynamic motivational speaker on the Women's Conference circuit. Committed to the advancement of strong, confident girls and women, she has dedicated much of her career to providing females of all ages with the tools necessary to succeed both personally and professionally.

Alethea's primary mission is to help young girls and women build their self-esteem and recognize the value they bring to the world around them.

Alethea holds a Bachelor's in Business Administration and a Master's in Education. She makes her home in Philadelphia, PA.